PRINT HANDWRITING WORKBOOK

ALPHABET, JOKES, FUNNY PHRASES AND MORE!

over 157 pages full of funny jokes and riddles for GIRLS!

Alex T. Howell
& Awesome Workbooks

Print Handwriting Workbook
Alphabet, Jokes, Funny Phrases and More!

Hello Future
Print Handwriting
Master!

We firmly believe that the art and skill of handwriting is both beautiful and important. We live in the digital age, but the most beautiful and important words are still written by hand.

Print is a handwriting style where letters appear to be disconnected. It can also be called block letters, print script, or manuscript. These handwriting styles are often used to write on official forms. This is because the cursive style of writing is harder to read.

What's more, writing by hand could make you smarter! Children who can write smoothly and clearly are better able to use writing to record thoughts and ideas. When your handwriting is automatic, your ideas can flow! To learn handwriting, you need to combine fine motor skills, language, memory and concentration. And we don't think you will deny that a handwritten letter is much more valuable and romantic than one that is printed or sent by e-mail!

It is also well known that play is the highest form of learning! That's why this workbook will guide you from the very beginning - from learning how to write single letters, to short words and writing whole sentences - in a fun and entertaining way.

Instead of rewriting boring sentences, you will practice on jokes! Instead of getting bored writing the same thing over and over again, you'll be copying and making up your own funny sentences. And as a break, you can play cryptogram! Sounds good, doesn't it?

So practice, copy, create, write, and remember to always have fun!

And here's what you'll find inside:

For each letter of the alphabet there are 6 pages full of interesting and entertaining exercises:

1. Single letter practice!

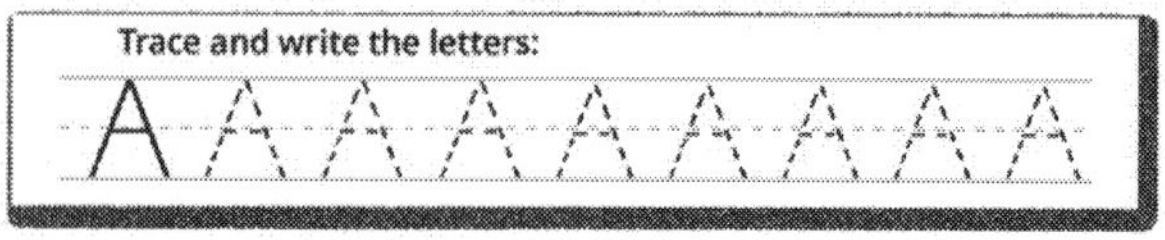

2. Joining letters!

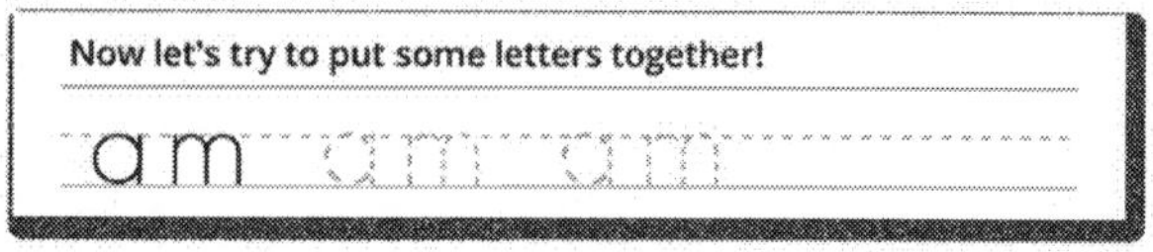

3. Writing short words!

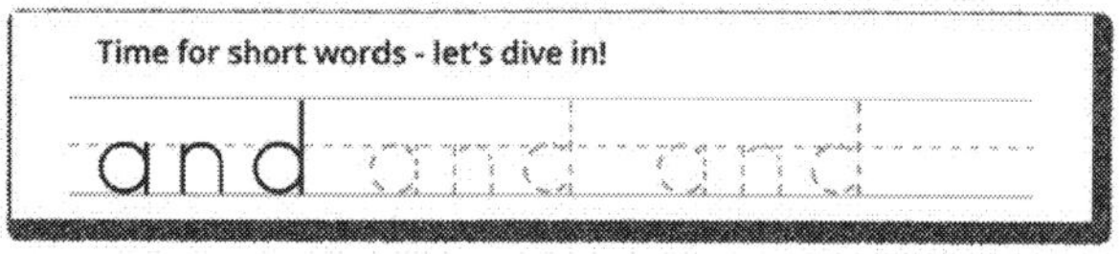

4. Copying funny sentences!

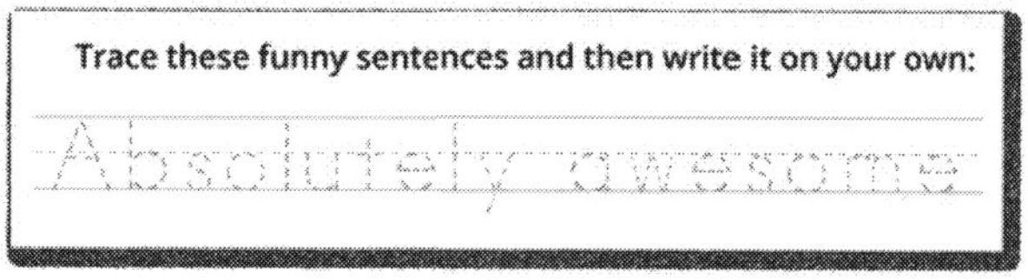

5. Funny cryptogram puzzles!

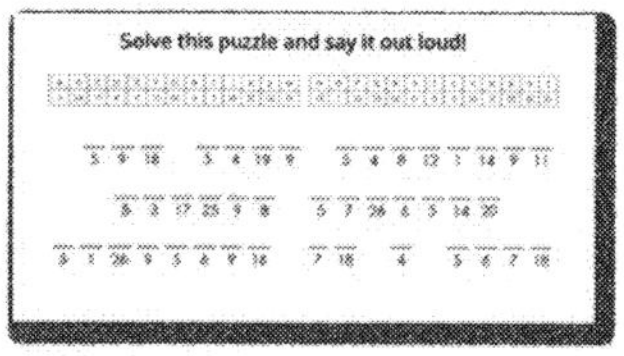

6. Tracing funny jokes!

7. Coming up with hilarious sentences!

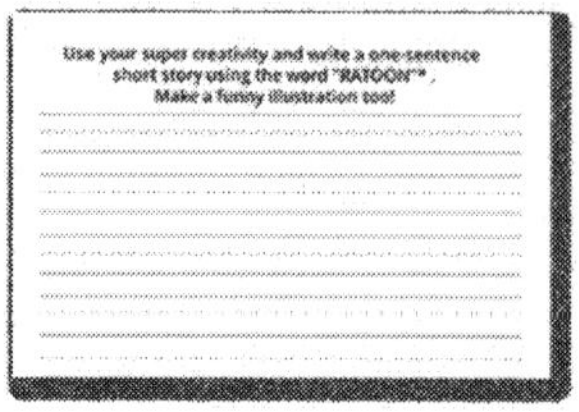

8. Extra page with creative writing prompt and space for drawing funny illustration!

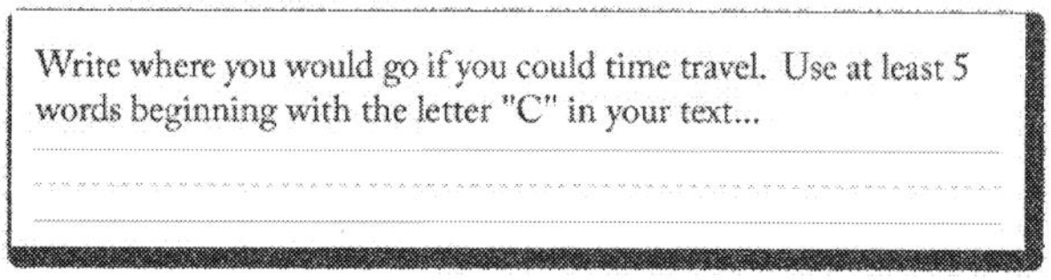

Some tips to help you start:

Above all, always remember to sit comfortably when writing. Place your feet flat on the floor, straighten your back, relax your shoulders - good posture is essential.

If you're using a pencil, choose a pencil with a soft B tip. If you prefer something else, a felt-tip pen or gel pen is best, as it has fluid delivery of ink and allows you to write smoothly.

Don't limit your exercises to paper only! Be creative, draw letters in the air, in the sand, on your friend's back - let them guess what you wrote! Make it fun and creative!

Remember to hold the pencil correctly. It is important that the tip of the thumb connects with the pencil. Only the correct grip will guarantee that in the future you will write quickly and fluently.

Each letter has up to six pages of exercises and each subsequent one is more difficult. Therefore, if you are just starting to learn print handwriting, we suggest first doing the first exercise for each letter, then the second one, and so on. It will be easier for you to first practice writing each letter separately, and only then teach your hand to write different letters in short words, and then in whole sentences. Good luck, future

Master of Print Handwriting

Currently, there are 65 different alphabets used worldwide. The richest of them is Khmer, which has 72 letters, while the most economical is the alphabet of one of the languages of Papua New Guinea, which requires only 11 letters.

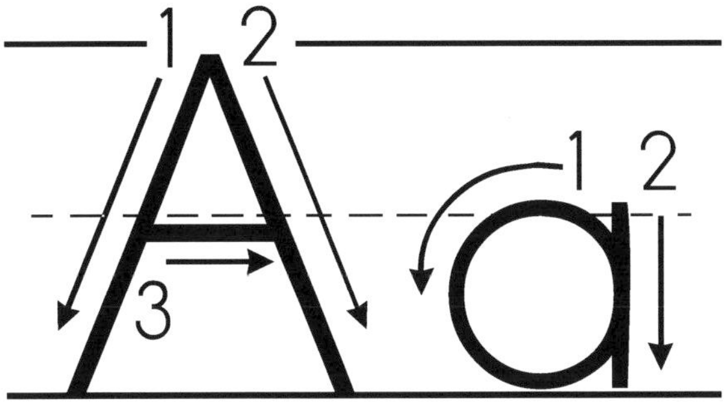

Trace and write the letters:

A A A A A A A A A A A A

A A

a a a a a a a a a a a a a a

a a

Now let's practice some more:

An An An

Ai Ai Ai

Ao Ao Ao

am am am

ac ac ac

ai ai ai

as as as

Time for short words - let's dive in!

Ace Ace Ace

Ape Ape Ape

Aid Aid Aid

ape ape ape

aid aid aid

arm arm arm

and and and

I want to write neatly because I keep a friendship journal in which my friend and I write notes to each other. We also draw in it, and sometimes we print photos and paste them inside.
(Amelia, age 11)

Trace these funny sentences and then write them on your own!

Absolutely awesome
alligators attempted
acrobatic antics.

An avocado
accidentally adorned
an anteater's ascot.

Trace these jokes and then write them on your own:

What's a gummy bear?
A bear with no teeth.

How does a penguin
build its house? Igloos
it together!

Ancient Egyptians used hieroglyphs, a complex system of pictorial symbols, for writing. They were inscribed on various surfaces, including temple walls and papyrus. The word "hieroglyph" comes from the Greek words "hieros" (sacred) and "glyphein" (to carve), emphasizing the sacred and artistic nature of these symbols. The ancient Egyptian hieroglyphic script consisted of over 7,000 different characters.

Use your super creativity and write a one-sentence short story using the word "**ABSQUATULATE.**"*

*Absquatulate means to leave abruptly or in a hurry, often in a comical context.

Solve this puzzle and say it out loud!

A	B	C	D	E	F	G	H	I	J	K	L	M	N	O	P	Q	R	S	T	U	V	W	X	Y	Z
24	1	20	2	4	12	7	10	21	19	11	18	9	13	8	16	6	17	14	3	22	25	23	15	5	26

24 13 5   13 8 21 14 4   24 13 13 8 5 14   24 13

8 5 14 3 4 17   1 22 3   24   13 8 21 14 5

13 8 21 14 4   24 13 13 8 5 14   24 13

8 5 14 3 4 17   9 8 17 4

Extra page in case you want to practice some more!

A is the first letter in the alphabet, isn't it? When was the last time when you did something for the first time? Write a short story about it. Use at least 5 words beginning with the letter "A" in your text...

...and draw a funny illustration!

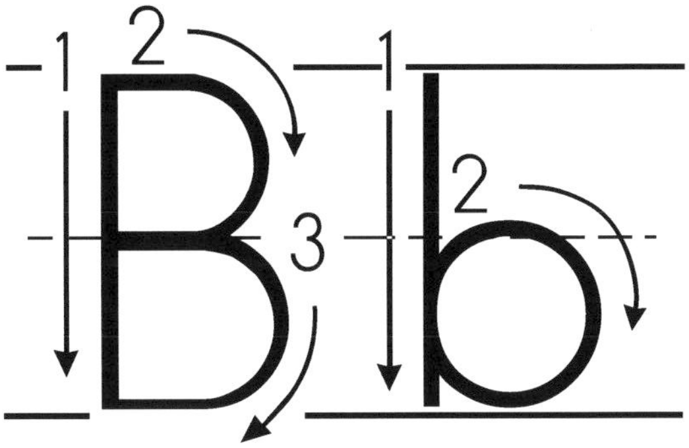

Trace and write the letters:

B B B B B B B B B B B B B

B B

b b b b b b b b b b b b b

b b

Now let's practice some more:

Be Be Be

Bi Bi Bi

Br Br Br

ba ba ba

bc bc bc

bi bi bi

bn bn bn

Time for short words - let's dive in!

Big Big Big

Bill Bill Bill

Bit Bit Bit

ball ball ball

bat bat bat

boy boy boy

box box box

Art is my favorite subject at school, and handwriting is like art, but with letters! You can make your words fancy or silly. It's like coloring, but with words, and you get to create your own masterpiece. I love that! (Ava, age 12)

Trace these funny sentences and then write them on your own!

Bobo the baboon
bought a bright blue
bouncy ball.

Ben's brother baked
buttery biscuits
before breakfast.

Trace these jokes and then write them on your own:

What do you call a fish with no eyes? Fsh!

What do unicorns eat for breakfast? Lucky charms!

China produces 38 billion pens every year - enough to give each person on Earth over 5 pens (80% of the world's pen production). Despite such enormous production, until recently, Chinese companies had to import pen tips from abroad because they did not have the technology to produce parts with sufficient precision.

Use your super creativity and write a one-sentence short story using the word "**BIBLIOPOLE.**"*

* Bibliopole is a person who collects or sells books, often with a sense of passion or humor about their collection.

Solve this puzzle and say it out loud!

A	B	C	D	E	F	G	H	I	J	K	L	M
18	13	3	8	2	22	26	25	4	5	21	6	1

N	O	P	Q	R	S	T	U	V	W	X	Y	Z
11	12	15	9	23	19	24	10	17	7	16	20	14

13 2 24 24 20 13 12 24 24 2 23 13 12 10 26 25 24

19 12 1 2 13 10 24 24 2 23 13 10 24

19 25 2 19 18 4 8 24 25 2

13 10 24 24 2 23 19 13 4 24 24 2 23

Extra page in case you want to practice some more!

Bibliopoles love books. Do you? What is your favorite book of all times? Write about one scene from your favorite book. Use at least 5 words beginning with the letter "B" in your text.

...and draw a funny illustration!

Cc

Trace and write the letters:

C

c

Now let's try to put some letters together!

Cy

Ce

Cr

ce ce ce

cd cd cd

cj cj cj

ca ca ca

Time for short words - let's dive in!

Can Can Can

Cake Cake Cake

Cell Cell Cell

cat cat cat

cow cow cow

cup cup cup

cot cot cot

I like to write down things that happen to me everyday, like a diary. I prefer to do it by hand, becuase it feels nice and because I can also draw things on the side. (Khloe, age 9)

Trace these funny sentences and then write them on your own!

Crazy cats carefully
caught colorful
candy canes.

Clumsy clowns
collided, causing
chaotic confusion.

Trace these jokes and then write them on your own:

Where does a mermaid sleep? A waterbed!

Why did the bicycle fall over? Because it was two-tired.

With a bit of imagination, you can use an ordinary pen (such as a Bic) to... lure termites out of the house. This is because some inks used in pens emit a scent identical to the pheromones that termites use to mark paths leading to food. When hungry, termites can just easily follow a path drawn with a pen by mistake.

Use your super creativity and write a one-sentence short story using the word **"CATTYWAMPUS."***

*Catywampus means askew, awry, kitty-corner. This word is a variant of catawampus, another example of great American slang from the 19th century. It can also mean "an imaginary fierce wild animal" or "savage, destructive."

Solve this puzzle and say it out loud!

A	B	C	D	E	F	G	H	I	J	K	L	M
18	12	6	23	22	20	4	17	1	10	15	7	9

N	O	P	Q	R	S	T	U	V	W	X	Y	Z
16	26	24	3	2	25	8	19	13	14	11	5	21

6 18 16   5 26 19   6 18 16   18   6 18 16

18 25   18   6 18 16 16 22 2   6 18 16

6 18 16   18   6 18 16

Extra page in case you want to practice some more!

Write where you would go if you could time travel. Use at least 5 words beginning with the letter "C" in your text...

...and draw a funny illustration!

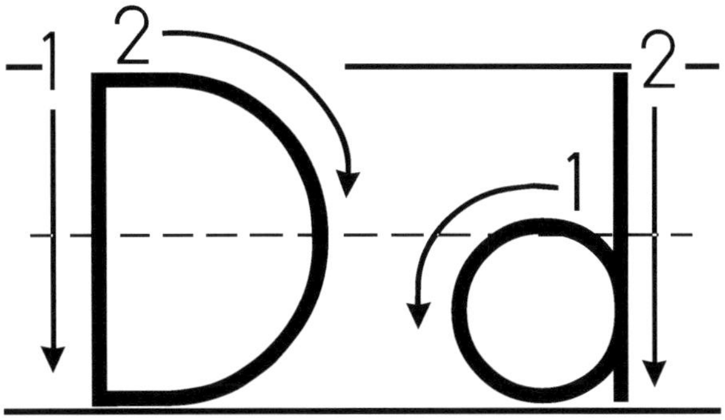

Trace and write the letters:

D D D D D D D D D D D D

D D

d d d d d d d d d d d d d

d d

Now let's practice some more:

De De De

Dr Dr Dr

Dg Dg Dg

dn dn dn

dj dj dj

dl dl dl

dh dh dh

Time for short words - let's dive in!

Dice Dice Dice

Den Den Den

Dig Dig Dig

deer deer deer

dog dog dog

dad dad dad

duck duck duck

Two weeks ago my grandma had birthday. She doesn't have a smartphone, and because I can write I could send her a birthday card by post. It was a surprise and she was very happy!
(Rosalie, age 12)

Trace these funny sentences and then write them on your own!

Dumb dutiful deer
dated a divine
dapper doberman.

Danny, the daring
duck, danced
a delightful disco.

Trace these jokes and then write them on your own:

Which state do
unicorns like most?
Maine.

What do you call a fake
noodle? An impasta!

Handwriting is never the same for two people, even for twins! Just like fingerprints and palm lines are unique, handwriting is also one-of-a-kind!

Use your super creativity and write a one-sentence short story using the word **"DOODLEBUG."***

*The word "doodlebug" can be used for any number of meanings from someone who simply likes to draw, to a person who wastes all sorts of time. The other most frequently used meaning of doodlebug is probably as a description of an actual insect. Doodlebugs, as they refer to an actual creature are usually associated with ant lions in their larval form.

Solve this puzzle and say it out loud!

A	B	C	D	E	F	G	H	I	J	K	L	M
5	14	11	16	7	26	2	10	4	1	22	25	24

N	O	P	Q	R	S	T	U	V	W	X	Y	Z
21	19	17	6	20	15	3	12	13	9	23	18	8

16 5 13 7 15   16 12 11 22   16 4 13 7 16   5 15

16 7 7 17   5 15   16 5 13 7 15   16 19 2

16 4 13 7 16

Extra page in case you want to practice some more!

Write about your perfect meal. It doesn't have to be real! Use at least 5 words beginning with the letter "D" in your text...

...and draw a funny illustration!

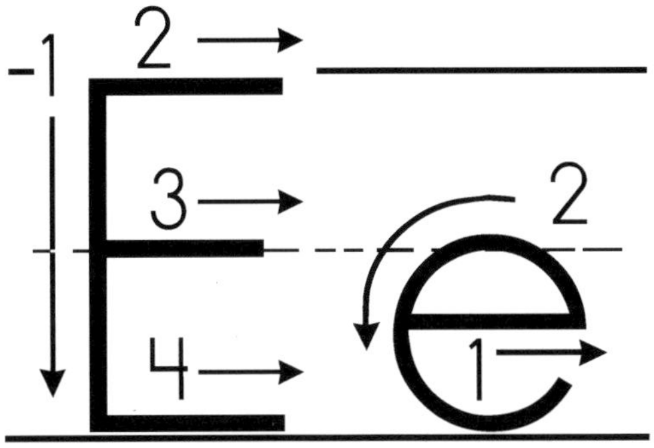

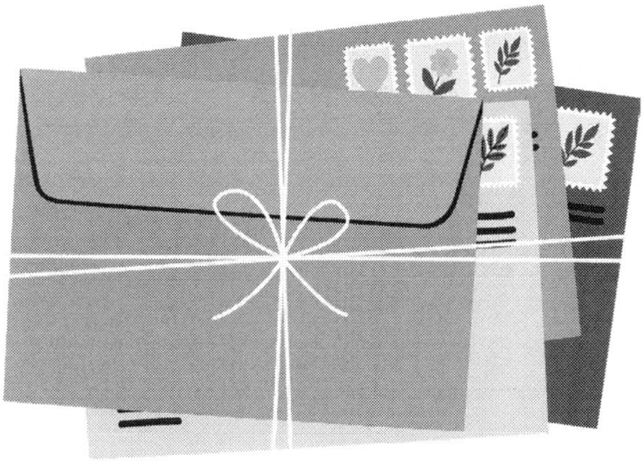

Trace and write the letters:

E

e

Now let's practice some more:

Eo

Es

Ey

ei ei ei

ey ey ey

eh eh eh

en en en

Time for short words - let's dive in!

Easy Easy Easy

Earn Earn

Eat Eat Eat

ear ear ear

end end end

egg egg egg

eye eye eye

I love making secret treasure maps with my handwriting. I hide them, and then my friends and I go on real treasure hunts, just like pirates! (Sara, age 11)

Trace these funny sentences and then write them on your own!

Eager elephants
eagerly eat
enormous eclairs.

Excited emus en-
thusiastically enjoyed
enormous eggplants.

Trace these jokes and then write them on your own:

Why did the scare-
crow win an award?
It was outstanding!

What fish costs the
most? A goldfish!

Research suggests that students who take notes by hand tend to retain information better than those who type their notes. The physical act of writing helps with information processing and retention.

Use your super creativity and write a one-sentence short story using the word "**ELEUTHEROMANIA.**"*

*Eleutheromania is an intense and irrational desire for freedom. The humorous aspect lies in the idea of being so passionate about freedom that it becomes a "mania."

Solve this puzzle and say it out loud!

A	B	C	D	E	F	G	H	I	J	K	L	M
17	7	15	14	4	16	24	22	18	9	11	19	25

N	O	P	Q	R	S	T	U	V	W	X	Y	Z
13	10	12	21	5	23	20	26	6	2	8	3	1

___ ___ ___ ___ ___ ___   ___ ___ ___ ___ ___ ___ ___ ___ ___ ___

4 19 4 6 4 13   7 4 13 4 6 10 19 4 13 20

___ ___ ___ ___ ___ ___ ___ ___ ___

4 19 4 12 22 17 13 20 23

Extra page in case you want to practice some more!

Imagine you are an elephant for one day. How would your day look like? Write about it and use at least 5 words beginning with "E" in your text.

...and draw a funny illustration!

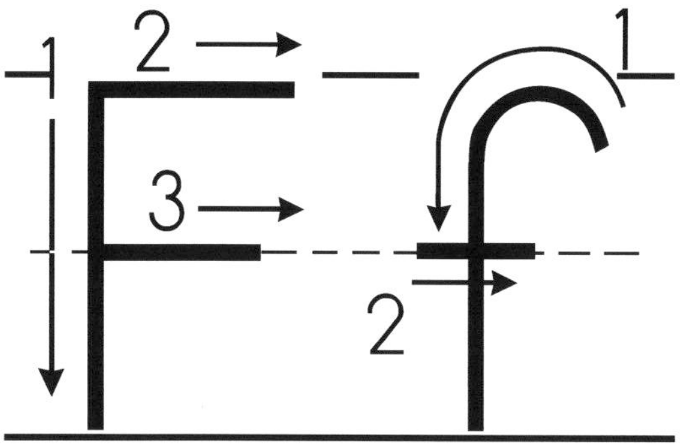

Trace and write the letters:

F F F F F F F F F F F F F

F F

f f f f f f f f f f f f f f

f f

Now let's practice some more:

Fn Fn Fn

Fi Fi Fi

Fe Fe Fe

fm fm fm

fc fc fc

ft ft ft

fo fo fo

Time for short words - let's dive in!

Fox Fox Fox

Fair Fair Fair

Fact Fact Fact

far far far

fill fill fill

feel feel feel

face face face

I always help my mom with the grocery list. I write down what we need to buy. It's like being a shopping superhero, making sure we get all the best snacks! (Faith, age 11)

Trace these funny sentences and then write them on your own!

Funny friendly
ferret faces
fascinating fear.

Fluffy fat flamingo
finds fabulous
fuchsia figs.

Trace these jokes and then write them on your own:

How do you make a tissue dance? Put a little boogie in it.

What falls but never gets hurt? Snow.

A graphologist analyzes handwriting and studies the relationship between its character, personality traits, and emotions. They do not require knowledge of a particular language (such as German or Japanese) when analyzing handwritten text.

Use your super creativity and write a one-sentence short story using the word **"FINIFUGAL."***

*You are finifugal if you're afraid of finishing something, you hate endings; it describes someone who tries to avoid or prolong the final moment of a story, relationship, or some other journey.

Solve this puzzle and say it out loud!

A	B	C	D	E	F	G	H	I	J	K	L	M
16	23	13	25	1	4	19	14	3	12	21	6	10

N	O	P	Q	R	S	T	U	V	W	X	Y	Z
24	7	5	18	17	15	8	26	11	20	9	2	22

4 7 26 17   4 3 24 1   4 17 1 15 14

4 3 15 14   4 7 17   2 7 26

Extra page in case you want to practice some more!

What makes you special and unique? Write about it and use at least 5 words beginning with the letter "F" in your text...

...and draw a funny illustration!

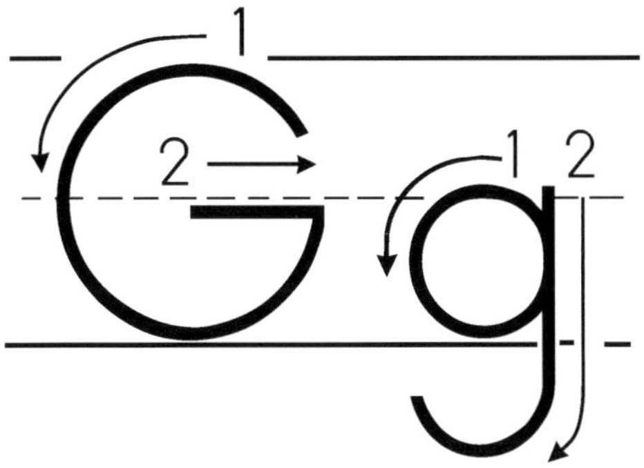

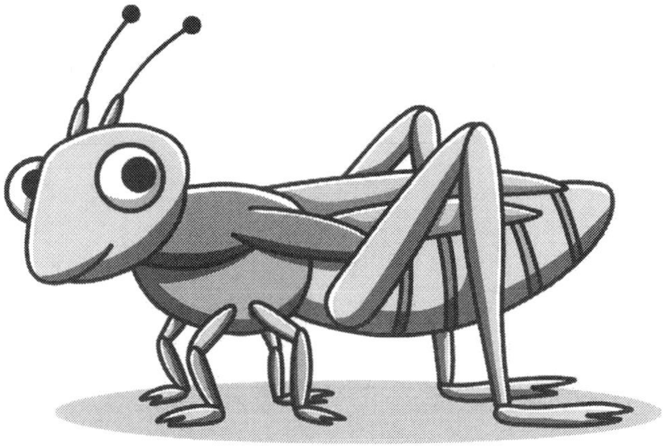

Trace and write the letters:

G G G G G G G G G G

G G

g g g g g g g g g g g g g

g g

Now let's practice some more:

Gn Gz Gz

Ge Ge Ge

Gr Gr Gr

gu gu gu

gh gh gh

gn gn gn

gt gt gt

Time for short words - let's dive in!

Gun Gun Gun

Goat Goat Goat

Girl Girl Girl

go go go

gem gem gem

gear gear gear

game game game

When I lost my first tooth I wrote a tiny note to the Tooth Fairy and left it under my pillow. The next morning, I found a shiny coin! Handwriting gets me magic visits! (Amy, 8)

Trace these funny sentences and then write them on your own!

Giggling gorillas
gracefully gobble
grapefruit.

Gleeful giraffes
gallop, grazing on
green grass.

Trace these jokes and then write them on your own:

Where do naughty unicorns go? Unicourt.

Why didn't the dog want to play foot-ball? It was a boxer!

Jane Austen, the renowned author of novels like "Pride and Prejudice" and "Sense and Sensibility," had exceptionally small and neat handwriting. Her letters were a model of penmanship. Austen's handwriting is often studied by scholars and enthusiasts, and her manuscripts provide valuable insights into her writing process and the meticulous care she took in crafting her novels.

Use your super creativity and write a one-sentence short story using the word **"GIBBERISH."***

*Gibberish means nonsense sounds or writing. An example of gibberish is a baby's babble. To gibber or to jabber is to talk rapidly and excitedly without making any sense.

Solve this puzzle and say it out loud!

A	B	C	D	E	F	G	H	I	J	K	L	M
8	6	7	24	2	19	15	17	3	9	4	26	21

N	O	P	Q	R	S	T	U	V	W	X	Y	Z
18	14	5	12	23	22	16	13	20	25	10	11	1

15 14 6 6 26 3 18 15   15 8 23 15 14 11 26 2 22

15 14 6 6 26 2 24   15 14 6 6 26 3 18 15

15 14 6 26 3 18 22

Extra page in case you want to practice some more!

You just ate a cookie that turned you 25 feet tall. What do you do next? Use at least 5 words beginning with the letter "G" in your text...

...and draw a funny illustration!

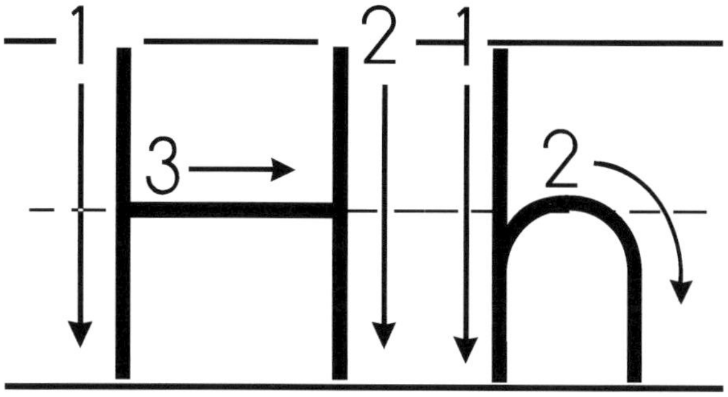

Trace and write the letters:

H H H H H H H H H H H

H H

h h h h h h h h h h h h h h

h h

Now let's practice some more:

Hn Hn Hn

Hi Hi Hi

Hl Hl Hl

he he he

ho ho ho

hr hr hr

hy hy hy

Time for short words - let's dive in!

Hug Hug Hug

Hole Hole Hole

Help Help Help

hot hot hot

hill hill hill

hat hat hat

hop hop hop

I hand-wrote a birthday card for my grandma, she was so happy!
(Diana, age 8)

Trace these funny sentences and then write them on your own!

Happy and hungry
hamster holds huge ham.

Hungry, hairy
hedgehogs hungrily
hunt hidden
huckleberries.

Trace these jokes and then write them on your own:

What is the parrot's favorite game? Hide and speak.

What's a slipper? A shoe made of a banana!

Hippopotomonstrosesquipedaliophobia means a fear of long words, which is quite ironic considering its own length. Feelings of shame or fear of ridicule for mispronouncing long words may cause distress or anxiety. Phobia isn't officially recognized as a diagnosis, so more research is needed.

Use your super creativity and write a one-sentence short story using the word **"HULLABALLOO."***

*Hullaballoo is an uproar or a noisy commotion, especially the sound of a bunch of people shouting in protest about something. It doesn't have to be literally noisy. "Hullaballoo" can also be used to name all the talk and commentary surrounding a controversy, such as on social media.

Solve this puzzle and say it out loud!

A	B	C	D	E	F	G	H	I	J	K	L	M
13	20	8	18	15	19	2	25	3	14	7	11	24

N	O	P	Q	R	S	T	U	V	W	X	Y	Z
23	5	16	22	4	17	1	9	10	12	6	21	26

25 13 4 4 21   1 25 15   25 9 23 2 4 21

25 9 23 2 4 21   25 3 16 16 5   3 17

25 13 16 16 3 11 21   15 13 1 3 23 2   25 13 24

Extra page in case you want to practice some more!

Imagine your best friend is a hippo. What would you ask him about? What would you tell him? Use at least 5 words beginning with the letter "H" in your text, write the questions down...

...and draw a funny illustration!

I i

Trace and write the letters:

I I I I I I I I I I I I I I I I I I I I I I

I I

i i i i i i i i i i i i i i i i i i i i i i i i i i i i i i

i i

Now let's practice some more:

In In In

Ii Ii Ii

Is Is Is

ik ik ik

io io io

ir ir ir

iw iw iw

Time for short words - let's dive in!

Ice Ice Ice

Iron Iron Iron

Ink Ink Ink

ire ire ire

ill ill ill

idle idle idle

ivy ivy ivy

I like to play boardgames, and recently, as I learn how to write and read, I started playing scrabble with my dad. He is still winning, but I'm becoming better and better at it! (Leah, age 9)

Trace these funny sentences and then write them on your own!

Intelligent iguana is inside impressive icy igloo.

Internet is insanely interesting innova-tion.

Trace these jokes and then write them on your own:

What was the unicorns favorite type of a story?

A fairy tail.

What room has no doors or windows? Mushroom.

Gutenberg invented printing, but it brought him... bankruptcy! The improvement and successful construction of a printing press, as well as the ambitious project of publishing a two-volume Bible, cost Gutenberg a total of 20,000 guilders in loans. The debt led to a lawsuit, bankruptcy, and the loss of his workshop.

Use your super creativity and write a one-sentence short story using the word "**INCOMPREHENSIBILE**"*.

*Incomprehensibile means to be very complex and difficult to understand.

Solve this puzzle and say it out loud!

A	B	C	D	E	F	G	H	I	J	K	L	M
4	14	9	16	10	1	13	5	19	15	25	23	2

N	O	P	Q	R	S	T	U	V	W	X	Y	Z
26	6	7	8	20	18	12	22	11	17	21	3	24

___ 19   ___ ___ ___ 10 4 12   ___ ___ ___ 10 10 23   ___ ___ ___ ___ ___ 17 5 19 23 10

___ ___ ___ 3 6 22   ___ ___ ___ ___ 7 10 10 23   ___ ___ ___ 10 10 23

Extra page in case you want to practice some more!

"I" is for... "intuition"! Do you know what intuition is? Ask your mum or dad when was the last time they listened to their intuition. Write it down, using at least 5 words beginning with the letter "I" in your text. Good luck!

Draw a funny illustration!

J j

Trace and write the letters:

J J J J J J J J J J J J J J

J J

j j j j j j j j j j j j j j j

j j

Now let's practice some more:

Ju Ju Ju

Jk Jk Jk

Jo Jo Jo

ja ja ja

ji ju ju

jy jy jy

jh jh jh

Time for short words - let's dive in!

Jam Jam Jam

Jade Jade Jade

Join Join Join

just just just

june june june

joke joke joke

joy joy joy

Handwriting helps me put my name on my books, folders, and school supplies. It's like saying, "This is mine, hands off!" in a friendly way. (Madison, age 12)

Trace these funny sentences and then write them on your own!

Jumping jaguars
joyfully jump, jiving
with jellybeans.

Jolly Jeff just
jiggles juicy
Jalapeno jam.

Trace these jokes and then write them on your own:

How does a hurricane see? With one eye.

Why was the mermaid embarrassed? She saw the ship's bottom!

According to the Guinness World Records, the most expensive book is "The Birds of America." The publication was created by American ornithologist and painter John James Audubon. Audubon's book is considered the most expensive in the world. It is estimated that a copy of "The Birds of America" costs even over 10 million dollars. Why? The work was published in only 119 copies, of which 108 are located in museums and libraries.

Use your super creativity and write a one-sentence short story using the word **"JACKANAPES."***

*Jackanapes is from the fifteenth century, and it's thought to come from the phrase "Jack of Naples," or to have some connection to the word apes. It's an old fashioned way to describe a cheeky or impertinent person, especially a young man. Your great-grandfather might shake his cane and yell, "Get off my lawn, you jackanapes!" when the neighbor kids lose their basketball in his yard.

Solve this puzzle and say it out loud!

A	B	C	D	E	F	G	H	I	J	K	L	M
7	8	3	4	14	19	10	15	22	16	24	23	6

N	O	P	Q	R	S	T	U	V	W	X	Y	Z
9	20	12	25	5	2	1	11	17	13	18	21	26

16 11 2 1 22 9   16 11 6 12 22 9 10

16 20 21 20 11 2   16 20 22 9 14 4   22 9

16 20 15 9 9 7 2   16 11 8 22 23 14 14

Extra page in case you want to practice some more!

You are the teacher for the day. What will you do in your lesson? Write about it and use at least 5 words beginning with the letter "J" in your text...

...and draw a funny illustration!

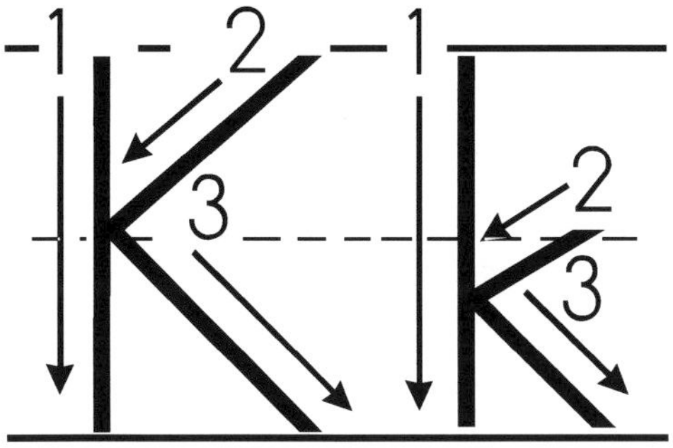

Trace and write the letters:

K

k

Now let's practice some more:

Kn

Ko

Kr

ki ki ki

ka ka ka

ky ky ky

ku ku ku

Time for short words - let's dive in!

Keg Keg Keg

Kept Kept Kept

Keen Keen Keen

kite kite kite

kiss kiss kidss

knot knot knot

king king king

Handwriting has been around for a long, long time, so when I write, it's like I'm connecting with the past. It's like a secret handshake with history! (Victoria, age 11)

Trace these funny sentences and then write them on your own!

Kids kindly kick
knitted, kinesthetic
kiwi.

Knight kidnapped
and kicked koala's
kidney.

Trace these jokes and then write them on your own:

What kind of eggs do monsters like? Terri-fried!

What does the dragon like to eat for a snack? Firecrackers!

In 1938, Hungarian journalist Laszlo Biro presented the world with a prototype of the ballpoint pen we know today. He improved on the technology of the ballpoint pen invented in the United States. The ink used in the pen smeared and spread, making it difficult to work with. Biro, who had already noticed that printing ink dried much faster and did not smear, prepared an ink with properties that combined both ink and paint with the help of his chemist brother. They also incorporated the ball mechanism from the pen design, which worked well for regulating ink flow in the pen.

Use your super creativity and write a one-sentence short story using the word **"KIBITZER."***

*KIBITIZER is a Yiddish word and is a synonym for a backseat driver. It can describe a person who is eager to give advice about something for which they are not responsible.

Solve this puzzle and say it out loud!

A	B	C	D	E	F	G	H	I	J	K	L	M
21	15	24	9	1	25	26	10	5	17	11	6	20

N	O	P	Q	R	S	T	U	V	W	X	Y	Z
7	3	16	22	4	19	18	2	14	8	23	13	12

11 1 7 7 13   5 19   5 7   18 10 1

11 5 18 24 10 1 7   1 21 18 5 7 26

11 5 18 11 21 18

Extra page in case you want to practice some more!

Imagine you're a magician and you need to create a magic elixir. What kind of potion are you going to create? What ingredients are you going to mix together? Describe it in the text below, using at least 5 letters beginning with the letter "K..."

...and draw a funny illustration!

L l

Trace and write the letters:

L

l

Now let's practice some more:

Li

Lu

Ly

le le le

lm lm lm

lk lk lk

ll ll ll

Time for short words - let's dive in!

Lock Lock Lock

Lyre Lyre Lyre

Lid Lid Lid

lolly lolly lolly

low low low

lion lion lion

love love love

I have a pen pal friend who lives abroad. She writes me handwritten letters, so I want to learn how to write back to her in the same way. Receiving letters is great! (Chloe, age 8)

Trace these funny sentences and then write them on your own!

Lanky llamas lighthe-
artedly leap, licking
lollipops.

Lively lemurs laugh
loudly, leaping like
lunatics.

Trace these jokes and then write them on your own:

What kind of pet did the mermaid have? A catfish.

Why did the cookie go to the doctor? It was feeling crumby.

Kubotan is a self-defense tool. It is a 14-centimeter rod carried as a keychain. It is designed for striking and pressing certain points on the body, such as the face, neck, larynx, nerve plexuses, or joints. It can also be used to strike bones. One type of kubotan is a tactical pen, which is a pen with additional functions. It is primarily disguised. Only people familiar with the topic will realize that we are not using an ordinary pen, but a self-defense accessory.

Use your super creativity and write a one-sentence short story using the word **"LOLLYGAG."***

*LOLLYGAG describes someone who is messing around and doing something that isn't useful.
For example: He goes to the beach to lollygag in the sun.

Solve this puzzle and say it out loud!

A	B	C	D	E	F	G	H	I	J	K	L	M
6	4	16	24	12	14	20	15	17	7	21	1	11

N	O	P	Q	R	S	T	U	V	W	X	Y	Z
3	18	2	26	23	5	9	8	13	10	22	19	25

__ __ __ __ __   __ __ __ __   __ __ __
1 6 23 23 19   5 12 3 9   9 15 12

__ __ __ __ __ __   __   __ __ __ __ __ __
1 6 9 9 12 23   6   1 12 9 9 12 23

__ __ __ __ __
1 6 9 12 23

Extra page in case you want to practice some more!

It started out just like an ordinary day, but then... Use at least 5 words beginning with the letter "L" in your text...

...and draw a funny illustration!

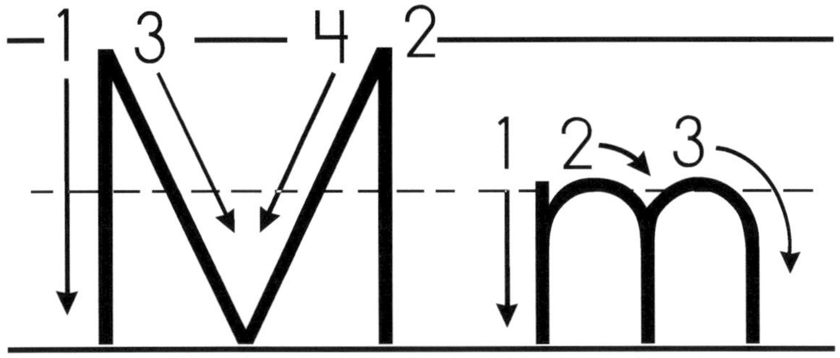

Trace and write the letters:

M M M M M M M M

M M

m m m m m m m m m m

m m

Now let's practice some more:

Mi Mi Mi

Ms Ms Ms

Mr Mr Mr

me me me

mk mk mk

mc mc mc

ma ma ma

Time for short words - let's dive in!

Mom Mom Mom

Mail Mail Mail

Mud Mud Mud

man man man

mole mole mole

moo moo moo

mat mat mat

I'm learning spanish at school, and sometimes I struggle to remember new words. My teacher told me to write them down several times in order to remember them better. It works! (Charlotte, age 7)

Trace these funny sentences and then write them on your own!

Mother mouse
makes marshmallow
macaroni.

Muttering mammoth
Mark makes
mortgages.

Trace these jokes and then write them on your own:

What fruit do scare-
crows love the most?
Straw-berries.

What looks like half a
unicorn? The other half.

The most expensive pen is the Heaven Gold - it cost one million dollars and was created by Anita Tan. It is made of 24-carat pink gold and adorned with 1888 diamonds weighing 48 carats. 161 of the diamonds have fancy colors, giving the pen a unique character.

Use your super creativity and write a one-sentence short story using the word **"MOLLYCODDLE."***

*MOLLYCODDLE means to spoil or overindulge something. You can think of mollycoddle as an extreme form of coddle. If you constantly fuss over your dog and serve her homemade food while she's resting on a soft feather bed, you mollycoddle her.

Solve this puzzle and say it out loud!

A	B	C	D	E	F	G	H	I	J	K	L	M
18	24	26	13	22	10	11	16	9	21	8	23	4

N	O	P	Q	R	S	T	U	V	W	X	Y	Z
17	12	6	3	25	5	15	20	19	7	14	2	1

__ __ __ __ __ __   __ __ __ __   __ __ __ __ __

4 9 11 16 15 2   4 9 8 22   4 18 8 22 5

__ __ __ __ __ __ __ __ __ __   __ __ __ __ __ __ __ __

4 18 25 19 22 23 23 12 20 5   4 20 17 26 16 9 22 5

__ __ __   __ __ __ __

10 12 25   4 18 25 2

Extra page in case you want to practice some more!

Imagine you are a bowl of oatmeal. What would you like to have inside you? Banana? Raisins? Write it down, using at least 5 words beginning with the letter "M" in your text...

...and draw a funny illustration!

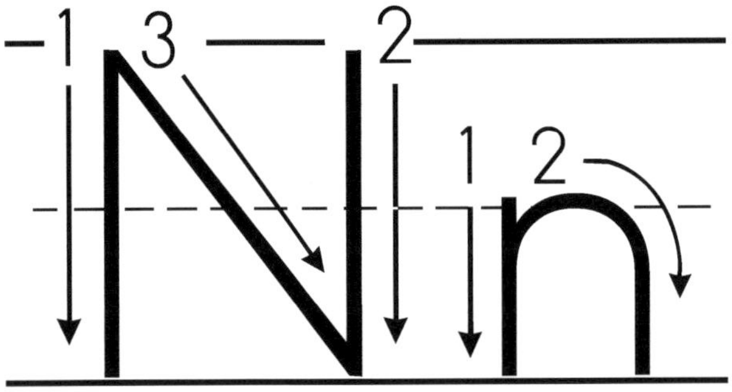

Trace and write the letters:

N N N N N N N N N N N

N N

n n n n n n n n n n n n n n

n n

Now let's practice some more:

Ne Ne Ne

Ni Ni Ni

Ny Ny Ny

no no no

na na na

nu nu nu

nh nh nh

Time for short words - let's dive in!

New New New

Nine Nine Nine

Ninja Ninja Ninja

nap nap nap

next next next

nail nail nail

neck neck neck

My mom bought many new plants for the house. Each of them needs different treatment, so I helped my mum by writing small papers with the name of the plant, and some tips of how to take care of it. I then glued them to each pot. My mom was delighted! (Sophia, age 11)

Trace these funny sentences and then write them on your own!

Nine nice, nifty
nuns need neon,
neat napkins.

Noisy naughty
narwhal Ned nagged
nine noble nutrias.

Trace these jokes and then write them on your own:

Who keeps the ocean clean? The mermaid.

Which part of the deck stinks the most? The poop deck.

The caps of pens have holes. They were introduced because of the large number of deaths due to choking on pen caps - about 100 people per year.

Use your super creativity and write a one-sentence short story using the word **"NINCOMPOOPERY."***

*NINCOMPOOPERY is a playful term used to describe foolish or silly behavior, often with a humorous and light-hearted connotation. For example: "They kicked out our competent people and posted nincompoops" or "They can call me a nincompoop if they like."

Solve this puzzle and say it out loud!

A	B	C	D	E	F	G	H	I	J	K	L	M
15	6	7	9	2	1	24	5	25	14	10	16	8

N	O	P	Q	R	S	T	U	V	W	X	Y	Z
17	20	22	4	11	19	3	12	26	13	21	18	23

__ __ __ __   __ __ __ __ __ __   __ __ __ __ __ __ __ __

17 25 17 2   17 25 8 6 16 2   17 20 6 16 2 8 2 17

__ __ __ __ __ __ __   __ __ __ __

17 25 6 6 16 2 9   17 12 3 19

Extra page in case you want to practice some more!

You are a crazy inventor. You were asked by the government of the US to create an invention that will change the life on the planet. What are you going to invent? Describe your invention in the text below, using at least 5 words beginning with the letter "N..."

...and draw a funny illustration!

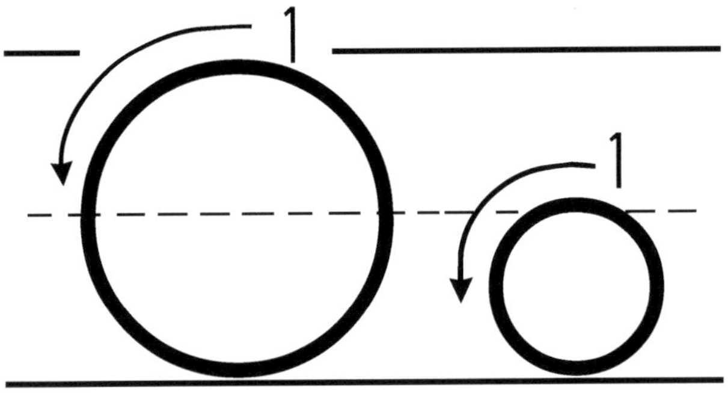

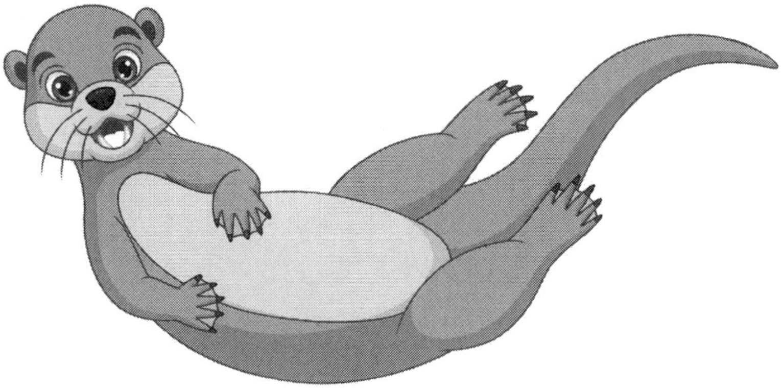

Trace and write the letters:

O

o

Now let's practice some more:

Ol

Op

Or

on on on

od od od

oh oh oh

ok ok okk

Time for short words - let's dive in!

Our Our Our

Old Old Old

Off Off Off

one one one

owl owl owl

oil oil oil

odd odd odd

Last month my class organised a special event at school and we needed to create a poster to promote it. My handwriting is very neat, so the teacher chose me to write the information on the poster. I was very proud of myself, seeing it every day on the school corridor! (Harper, age 12)

Trace these funny sentences and then write them on your own!

Outgoing otters

obsessed with

original oatmeal.

Odd optimistic owl

in orange onsie

orders olives.

Trace these jokes and then write them on your own:

What card game do
unicorns play? Uno.

What do you get if
you cross a unicorn and
a cow? Horned beef.

The Rotokas alphabet of Papua New Guinea has only 12 letters, making it one of the world's shortest alphabets. This compact alphabet is perhaps the smallest in use, with only 12 letters of ISO basic Latin alphabet without any diacritics and ligatures. The letters are A E G I K O P R S T U V. T and S both represent the phoneme /t/.

Use your super creativity and write a one-sentence short story using the word "ONOMATOPOEIA."*

*ONOMATOPOEIA refers to words that imitate or suggest the sound they describe. It is a word that actually looks like the sound it makes, and we can almost hear those sounds as we read. Here are some words that are used as examples of onomatopoeia: slam, splash, bam, babble, warble, gurgle, mumble, and belch. But there are hundreds of such words!

Solve this puzzle and say it out loud!

A	B	C	D	E	F	G	H	I	J	K	L	M
23	18	3	13	2	4	21	25	1	6	10	5	7

N	O	P	Q	R	S	T	U	V	W	X	Y	Z
16	11	12	9	22	15	26	24	14	17	20	19	8

___ ___ ___   ___ ___ ___   ___ ___ ___ ___ ___

11 13 13   11 5 13   11 5 5 1 2

___ ___ ___ ___   ___ ___ ___ ___   ___ ___ ___ ___ ___

11 1 5 15   11 1 5 19   23 24 26 11 15

Extra page in case you want to practice some more!

You have $1000 to spend. What will you buy? Use at least 5 words beginning with the letter "O" in your text...

...and draw a funny illustration!

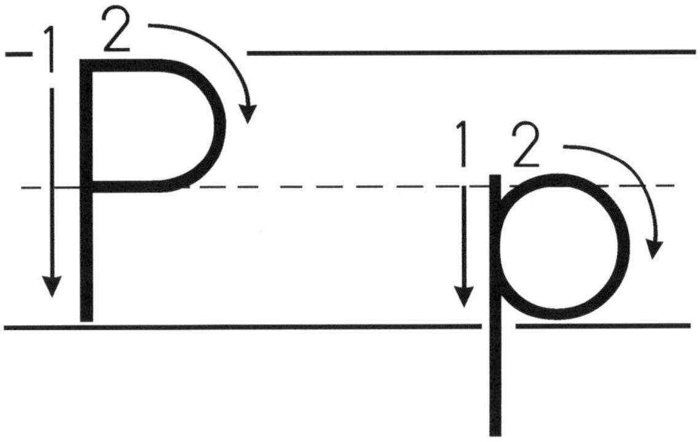

Trace and write the letters:

P P P P P P P P P P P P

P P

p p p p p p p p p p p p

p p

Now let's practice some more:

Po Po Po

Pl Pl Pl

Pi Pi Pi

pr pr pr

ps ps ps

pm pm pm

pp pp pp

Time for short words - let's dive in!

Past Past Past

Pie Pie Pie

Pen Pen Pen

post post post

play play play

pad pad pad

pet pet pet

I use my handwriting to write down the exciting discoveries I make during science experiments. It's like being a mad scientist with my lab notes! (Grace, age 11)

Trace these funny sentences and then write them on your own!

Poor plan – poor performance.

Pretty powerful parrot playfully pushed prudent princess.

Trace these jokes and then write them on your own:

How do trees usually get on the Internet?

They log in!

What's a seafood diet?

You see food & you eat it.

Pens created for astronauts have special properties. They work underwater, in a vacuum and on oily surfaces, and additionally last three times longer than regular pens.

Use your super creativity and write a one-sentence short story using the word "**PUMPERNICKEL.**"*

*PUMPERNICKEL is a type of dark, dense bread with a name that can be quite amusing and whimsical to say.

Solve this puzzle and say it out loud!

A	B	C	D	E	F	G	H	I	J	K	L	M
12	18	2	20	15	5	21	17	22	14	8	25	3

N	O	P	Q	R	S	T	U	V	W	X	Y	Z
16	6	26	4	24	13	19	11	10	9	23	1	7

26 15 19 15 24   26 22 26 15 24   26 22 2 8 15 20

12   26 15 2 8   6 5   26 22 2 8 25 15 20

26 15 26 26 15 24 13

Extra page in case you want to practice some more!

If you had a cap of inivisibility for one day, where would you go? What would you do? Write it down, using at least 5 words beginning withht he letter "P" in your text...

...and draw a funny illustration!

Q q

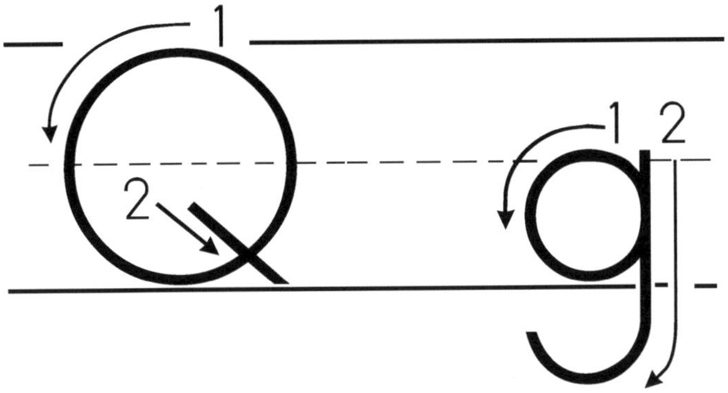

Trace and write the letters:

Q

q

Now let's practice some more:

Qn

Qu

Qa

qe qe qe

qw qw qw

qc qc qd

ql ql ql

Time for short words - let's dive in!

Quack Quack Quack

Quote Quote Quote

Quick Quick Quick

quit quit quit

quad quad quad

quiz quiz quiz

quiet quiet quiet

I created a handmade gift for my friend and included a handmade card. It turned out great and my friend was impressed! (Elizabeth, age 12)

Trace these funny sentences and then write them on your own!

Quirky qualified queen quits quiet quilting.

Quokkas quarter quickly quaintly quacks quotes.

Trace these jokes and then write them on your own:

What do English merma-
ids eat? Fish and ships.

What does a shark like to
eat with peanut butter?
Jellyfish!

Even the ancient Egyptians used reed "pens" for writing on papyrus. Predecessors to modern pens, now rarely used, included bird feathers, reed pens, fountain pens, and brushes.

Use your super creativity and write a one-sentence short story using the word **"QUIZZACIOUSLY."***

*QUIZZACIOUSLY means in a mocking or teasing manner. It's often used humorously to describe how someone is making fun of another person in a playful way.

Solve this puzzle and say it out loud!

A	B	C	D	E	F	G	H	I	J	K	L	M
4	6	22	11	25	7	15	13	12	14	10	3	2

N	O	P	Q	R	S	T	U	V	W	X	Y	Z
1	19	5	26	18	20	23	21	8	17	24	9	16

23 13 25   26 21 25 25 1   22 19 12 1 25 11

26 21 12 22 10   22 3 12 5 5 25 11

26 21 12 5 20

Extra page in case you want to practice some more!

Create a QUIZ. Think of 1 funny question, and write down three possible answers; two of them should be false and one true. Then ask the questions to your parents, friends or siblings. Use at least 5 words beginning with the letter "Q"...

...and draw a funny illustration!

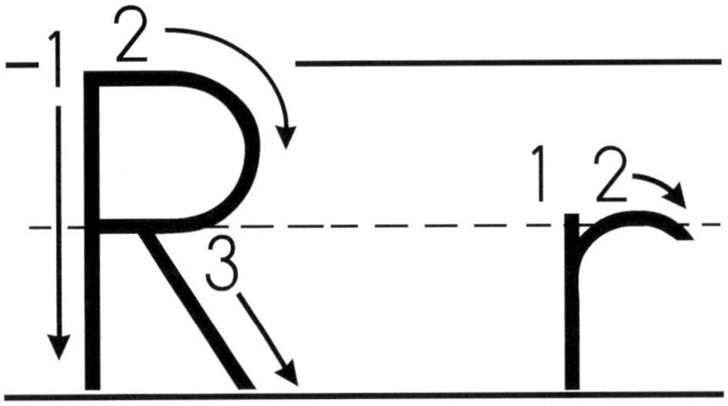

Trace and write the letters:

R

r

Now let's practice some more:

Re

Ry

Rd

rg rg rg

rh rh rh

ra ra ra

ru ru ru

Time for short words - let's dive in!

Roll Roll Roll

Rice Rice Rice

Race Race Race

rug rug rug

rare rare rare

run run run

rock rock rock

My teacher was so impressed with my handwriting that she specifically spoke to my mother after class to tell her about it. I saw that my mother was proud and happy!
(Camila, age 11)

Trace these funny sentences and then write them on your own!

Red, robust, reliable
rabbits run really
rapidly.

Ripe, reverent, rural
roses rarely
reservedly reek.

Trace these jokes and then write them on your own:

What color do kittens
love the most? Purrple.

What did the ocean say
to the beach?
Nothing, it just waved.

The Morse code was named after the inventor of the telegraph - Samuel Morse. It is an international code consisting of 26 letters from A to Z. There is no differentiation between upper and lower case letters in this notation. The most commonly used distress signal is SOS (three dots, three dashes, and three dots). It is used all over the world. The SOS signal was first used by the German naval infantry in 1904. The duration of a dash is equivalent to that of three dots.

Use your super creativity and write a one-sentence short story using the word "**RODOMONTADE.**"*

*RODOMONTADE (which can also be spelled rhodomontade) refers to boastful or bragging speech or behavior, often used humorously to describe someone who's excessively self-promoting or exaggerating their abilities. For example: "Anna amused him with some rodomontade about despising cartoons and comics."

Solve this puzzle and say it out loud!

A	B	C	D	E	F	G	H	I	J	K	L	M
5	21	7	26	24	1	11	25	17	2	19	20	23

N	O	P	Q	R	S	T	U	V	W	X	Y	Z
8	3	22	15	10	14	16	12	4	13	6	18	9

__ __ __ __ __   __ __ __ __   __ __ __ __
10 3 10 18 14   20 5 13 8   10 5 19 24

__ __ __ __ __ __   __ __ __ __ __
10 5 10 24 20 18   10 5 19 24 14

__ __ __ __ __ __   __ __ __ __ __
10 24 5 20 20 18   10 17 11 25 16

Extra page in case you want to practice some more!

A courier has just delivered you a mysterious box. What's inside? Use at least 5 words beginning with the letter "R" in your text...

...and draw a funny illustration!

S s

Trace and write the letters:

S S S S S S S S S S S S S S

S S

s s s s s s s s s s s s s s s s s

s s

Now let's practice some more:

Se Se Se

Sc Sc Sc

Sn Sn Sn

sa sa sa

sd sd sd

sg sg sg

si si si

Time for short words - let's dive in!

Sad Sad Sad

Sky Sky Sky

Six Six Six

salt salt salt

star star star

sun sun sun

silk silk silk

I used my handwriting skills and wrote a poem for my mom on Mother's Day, and she cried tears of joy! (Isabella, age 9)

Trace these funny sentences and then write them on your own!

Sweet, stylish Sally
sings sad sassy
songs.

Skilled Sam
suprisingly slapped
Simon's shiny scalp.

Trace these jokes and then write them on your own:

When does a horse talk?

Whinney wants to!

What Ipad says to the dentist? Help, I have a bluetooth!

In 1949, Marcel Bich created the first ballpoint pen available to the mass market. He named it "Bic" after his own surname. An average BIC pen can draw a continuous line that is 2 kilometers long.

Use your super creativity and write a one-sentence short story using the word "SUPERCALIFRAGILISTICEXPIALIDOCIOUS."*

*SUPERCALIFRAGILISTICEXPIALIDOCIOUS is a fictional word from the movie "Mary Poppins." It is used to describe something extraordinary.

Solve this puzzle and say it out loud!

A	B	C	D	E	F	G	H	I	J	K	L	M
1	25	20	19	6	11	12	17	21	8	10	5	7

N	O	P	Q	R	S	T	U	V	W	X	Y	Z
15	24	3	16	23	22	18	9	26	13	4	2	14

___ ___ ___   ___ ___ ___ ___   ___ ___ ___ ___ ___
22 21 4   22 21 20 10   17 21 20 10 22

___ ___ ___ ___ ___   ___ ___ ___   ___ ___ ___ ___ ___
15 21 20 10 22   22 21 4   22 5 21 20 10

___ ___ ___ ___ ___ ___   ___ ___ ___ ___   ___ ___ ___ ___ ___
25 23 21 20 10 22   13 21 18 17   3 21 20 10 22

Extra page in case you want to practice some more!

Create your own word, try to make it long and funny. Then write down the definition of this word and examples of situations in which you can use it. Use at least 5 words beginning with the letter "S" in your text...

...and draw a funny illustration!

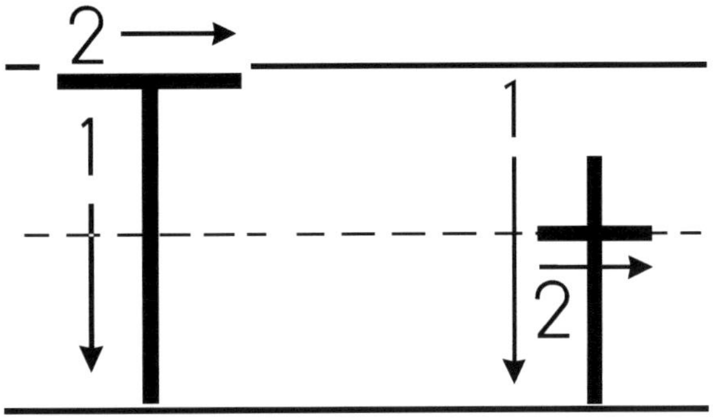

Trace and write the letters:

T

t

Now let's practice some more:

Tn

Tr

Ts

tm tm tm

to to to

tl tl tl

tt tt tt

Time for short words - let's dive in!

Tell Tell Tell

Toe Toe Toe

Top Top Top

tea tea tea

tall tall tall

tan tan tan

tip tip tip

I wanted to write a Valentine's Day letter to my crush. I used my handwriting skills and it came out very romantic, and well... we've already been on three dates! (Olivia, age 12)

Trace these funny sentences and then write them on your own!

Teal turtles travelled
tirelessly through the
tundra.

Tender tigers
thanked their tall,
tenacious, teachers.

Trace these jokes and then write them on your own:

What does one pirate say to his friend? I sea you!

How do clams call their friends? On their shell phones!

The French novelist Marcel Proust had an elegant and meticulous handwriting style. His intricate script was reflective of his meticulous attention to detail in his novels. Proust often wrote in green ink, which is not the most common color for writing. Additionally, he typically wrote on lined paper, which is different from the blank sheets many writers and novelists prefer.

Use your super creativity and write a one-sentence short story using the word **"TARADIDDLE."***

*TARADIDDLE is used when you want to explain that something someone is talking about is a childlish lie, over-exaggerated or pretentious nonsense. For example: "Yesterday she told me taradiddle about having, working quite a lot."

Solve this puzzle and say it out loud!

A	B	C	D	E	F	G	H	I	J	K	L	M
4	24	17	8	9	15	26	6	7	22	25	14	19

N	O	P	Q	R	S	T	U	V	W	X	Y	Z
18	1	12	13	16	11	5	3	10	2	23	20	21

_ _ _   _ _ _ _   _ _ _ _ _ _ _ _
5 9 18   5 4 19 9   5 4 8 12 1 14 9 11

_ _ _ _ _ _   _ _ _ _ _ _ _
5 3 17 25 9 8   5 7 26 6 5 14 20

_ _ _ _ _ _ _ _   _ _   _   _ _ _ _
5 1 26 9 5 6 9 16   7 18   4   5 6 7 18

Extra page in case you want to practice some more!

Would you rather be a turkey or a turtle? Why? Use at least 5 words beginning with the letter "T" in your text...

...and draw a funny illustration!

U u

Trace and write the letters:

U

u

Now let's practice some more:

Un

Us

Up

um um um

uc uc uc

uj uj uj

uo uo uo

Time for short words - let's dive in!

Ups Ups Ups

Undo Undo Undo

Urge Urge Urge

use use use

udon udon udon

user user user

unit unit unit

I personalize my school binder with my name and cool designs in my handwriting. It's like giving my binder a makeover, and it feels so unique. Everyone knows it's mine! (Evelyn, age 10)

Trace these funny sentences and then write them on your own!

Urban unicorns use
unique umber
umbrellas.

Ugly, unlucky urial
is ultimately upset.

Trace these jokes and then write them on your own:

What's a cat's favorite cereal? Mice Krispies.

What do you call a horse that lives next door? Your neigh-bor!

The word "pen" comes from the Latin word "penna," meaning feather. Humans used feathers that had sharpened quills for writing and began calling them pens.

Use your super creativity and write a one-sentence short story using the word **"UFOLOGY."***

*UFOLOGY is the study and investigation of UFOs or unidentified flying objects.

Solve this puzzle and say it out loud!

A	B	C	D	E	F	G	H	I	J	K	L	M
3	16	19	2	4	15	8	25	13	18	11	7	10

N	O	P	Q	R	S	T	U	V	W	X	Y	Z
9	22	23	20	14	17	1	21	6	24	12	5	26

3 9   21 9 2 4 14 1 3 11 4 14

21 9 2 4 14 1 22 22 11   1 22   21 9 2 4 14 1 3 11 4

3 9   21 9 2 4 14 1 3 11 13 9 8

Extra page in case you want to practice some more!

What if you could bring any animal to school? Use at least 5 words beginning with the letter "U" in your text...

...and draw a funny illustration!

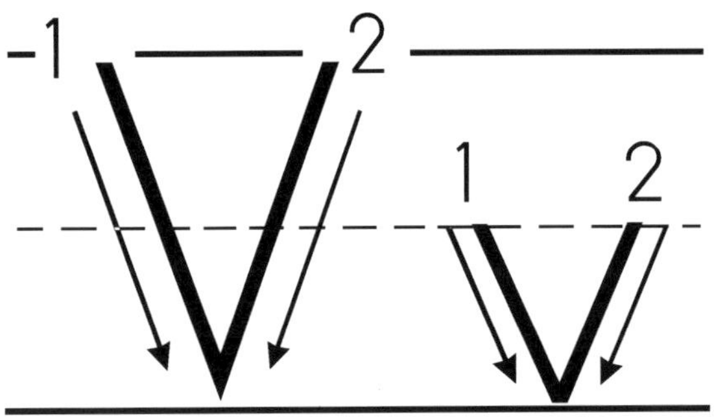

Trace and write the letters:

V

v

Now let's practice some more:

Vn

Vd

Va

vi vi vi

ve ve ve

vl vl vl

vj vj vj

Time for short words - let's dive in!

Van Van Van

Video Video Video

Vet Vet Vet

vow vow vow

vibe vibe vibe

very very very

vox vox vox

My teacher asked me to write the class schedule on the board, and everyone thought it looks really cool! (Avery, age 9)

Trace these funny sentences and then write them on your own!

Violet, vigilant vampire visited vast vulcano.

Vesicular, vibrant, vital virus varies violently.

Trace these jokes and then write them on your own:

How did the phone propose to its love? It gave her a ring.

What snakes are found on cars? Windshield vipers.

Some cultures and communities have a strong oral tradition, where stories, histories, and knowledge are passed down through spoken language rather than through written texts. In such cases, there may be little or no need for a writing system.

Use your super creativity and write a one-sentence short story using the word **"VEXED."***

*VEXED means that something is difficult and problematic. It also means to be annoyed, frustrated or worried. For example: "I'm very vexed with my cat!."

Solve this puzzle and say it out loud!

A	B	C	D	E	F	G	H	I	J	K	L	M
16	19	3	15	25	24	22	7	26	17	2	5	10

N	O	P	Q	R	S	T	U	V	W	X	Y	Z
4	21	1	9	14	6	23	13	11	8	20	18	12

__ __ __ __ __ __ __ __ __ __ __ __
11 26 4 3 25 4 23   11 21 8 25 15

__ __ __ __ __ __ __ __ __
11 25 4 22 25 16 4 3 25

__ __ __ __ __ __ __ __ __ __ __ __ __ __
11 25 14 18   11 25 7 25 10 25 4 23 5 18

Extra page in case you want to practice some more!

Do you believe in vampires? How would you behave if you saw one? Write down all the practical tips in case of a potential encounter with a vamipre. Use at least 5 words beginning with the letter "V" in your text...

...and draw a funny illustration!

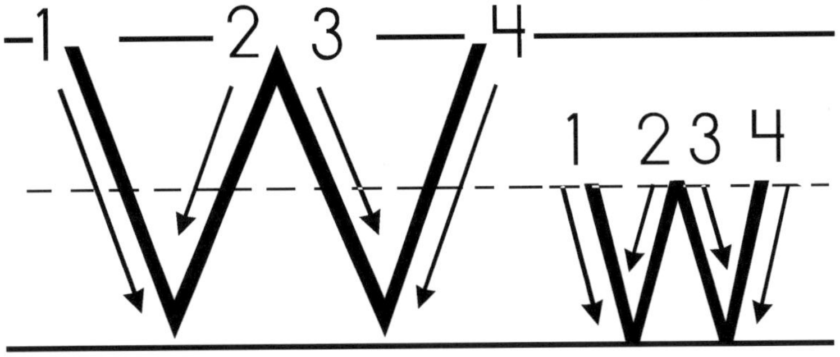

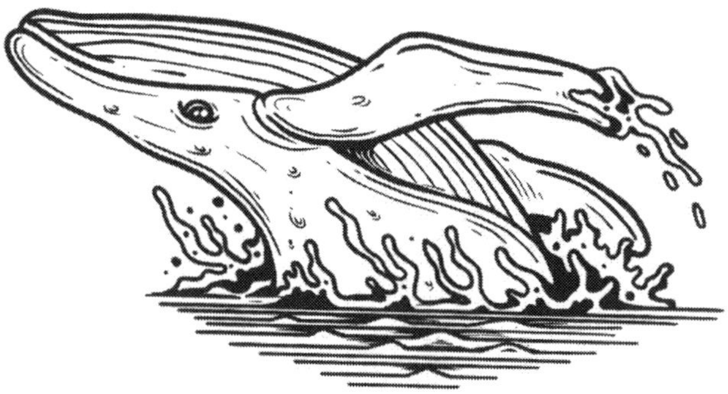

Trace and write the letters:

W W W W W W W W

W W

w w w w w w w w w w w w w w

w w

Now let's practice some more:

Wi Wi Wi

Ws Ws Ws

Wf Wf Wf

wg wg wg

wh wh wh

wa wa wa

we we we

Time for short words - let's dive in!

Wed Wed Wed

Wee Wee Wee

Wry Wry Wry

why why why

who who who

wet wet wet

wow wow wow

Our biology teacher gave us a task to collect different autumn leaves and write down the names of the trees they belong to. My handwriting is very neat and beautiful, so I made an amazing poster out of it! (Amelia, age 10)

Trace these funny sentences and then write them on your own!

Wobbly weasels
wiggle when whistling
whimsical waltzes.

Wet, watchful
wolves walk the
wrong way.

Trace these jokes and then write them on your own:

What is a pirate's
favorite fish? Swordfish!

What is the name of
the Subaru that fell into
a lake? Scubaru.

Gold-nibbed fountain pens can adapt to your writing style. It happens due to gold being a soft metal. The gold nib flexes and softens when used. Quill pens made of bird feathers were all the rage from 700 AD to 1700s. The best quills were made from swan feathers and were rare and expensive. So common folks used goose feather quills and got crow feather quills for making fine lines.

Use your super creativity and write a one-sentence short story using the word **"WADDLE."***

*WADDLE means to walk with short steps, swaying from side to side like a duck, penguin, or other animals with a distinctive gait, which can be quite comical to observe and describe.

Solve this puzzle and say it out loud!

A	B	C	D	E	F	G	H	I	J	K	L	M
24	22	23	21	20	1	2	3	9	6	15	19	7

N	O	P	Q	R	S	T	U	V	W	X	Y	Z
17	5	11	12	8	4	25	10	16	13	14	18	26

13 20 25 25 20 8   13 20 24 25 3 20 8   17 20 16 20 8

13 20 24 25 3 20 8 20 21   13 20 25 25 20 8

13 20 24 25 3 20 8   22 20 25 25 20 8

Extra page in case you want to practice some more!

Imagine you are a penguin, living on the North Pole. Describe one day of your life. Remember to use at least 5 letters beginning with the letter "W" in your text...

...and draw a funny illustration!

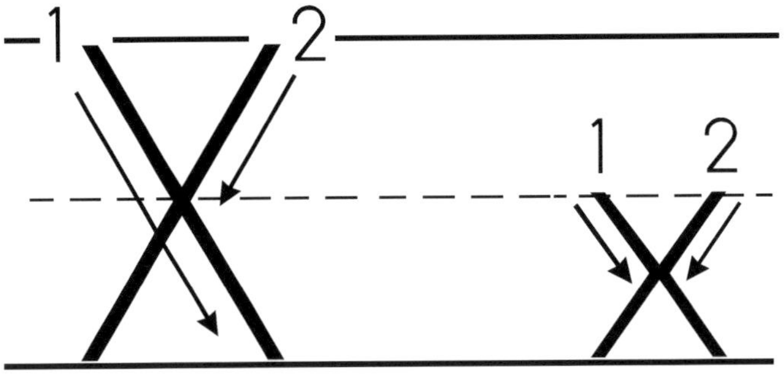

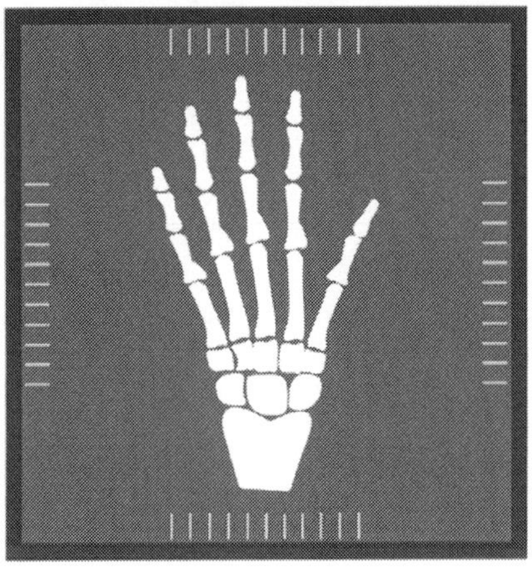

Trace and write the letters:

X X X X X X X X X X X

X X

x x x x x x x x x x x x x x x x x

x x

Now let's practice some more:

Xe Xe Xe

Xd Xd Xd

Xi Xi Xi

xo xo xo

xa xa xa

xj xj xj

xr xr xr

Time for short words - let's dive in!

XOXO XOXO XOXO

XD XD XD

Xenic Xenic Xenic

xxx xxx xxx

x-ray x-ray x-ray

xerox xerox xerox

xyst xyst xyst

I wanted to impress my te Last Christmas my mom asked me to help her pack the gifts for the rest of the family. I helped her pack them and then I wrote the names of the family members on the tags. It looked amazing! (Zoe, age 11)

Trace these funny sentences and then write them on your own!

Xavier has Xanax
and xenogenic
xenophobia.

Xylophone-playing
xenophobes exchange
xenon xenophones.

Trace these jokes and then write them on your own:

How does a skeleton call his friends? On the tele-bone.

What is the robot's favo-rite snack? Micro-chips.

English is the official language of airspace. This means that aviation personnel and airport staff must communicate in English. This is why the pilot and crew always speak English fluently, regardless of where they are flying from and to.

Use your super creativity and write a one-sentence short story using the word **"XERTZ."***

*XERTZ is pronounced "zerts." It means to gulp something down quickly and/or in a greedy way. In most cases, it is used to describe drinking, but it may also describe someone eating quickly. Example sentence: "I was thirsty and I needed to xertz a bottle of water."

Solve this puzzle and say it out loud!

A	B	C	D	E	F	G	H	I	J	K	L	M
6	7	15	19	14	26	13	20	25	10	18	9	8

N	O	P	Q	R	S	T	U	V	W	X	Y	Z
2	1	22	4	16	24	12	23	3	5	21	17	11

___ ___ ___ ___ ___ ___   ___ ___ ___ ___ ___ ___ ___ ___
21 6 2 19 14 16   14 21 6 8 25 2 14 24

___ ___ ___ ___ ___ ___ ___ ___ ___ ___   ___ ___ ___ ___ ___
21 17 9 1 22 20 1 2 14 24   5 20 25 9 14

___ ___ ___ ___ ___ ___ ___ ___   ___ ___ ___ ___ ___
21 14 16 1 21 25 2 13   21 16 6 17 24

Extra page in case you want to practice some more!

Have you ever heard about a dinosaur called Xenox? Well, if you haven't, that's not a problem. Let's just imagine what it looks like. Describe it in your text. If you run out of words starting with the letter "X," come up with your own new words...

...and draw a funny illustration!

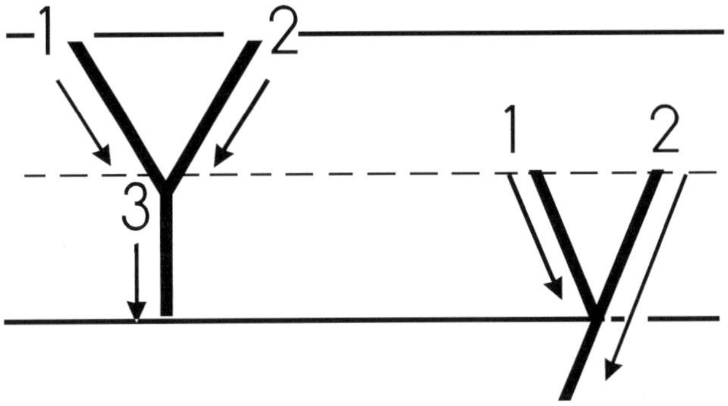

Trace and write the letters:

Y

y

Now let's practice some more:

Yu

Ys

Yn

yo yo yo

ya ya ya

ye ye ye

ym ym ym

Time for short words - let's dive in!

Yet Yet Yet

You You You

Yeti Yeti Yeti

yes yes yes

yup yup yup

yuck yuck yuck

yoyo yoyo yoyo

I practiced handwriting every day, and now I can write faster and neater!
(Natalie, age 10)

Trace these funny sentences and then write them on your own!

Young yak
yanked yellow
yearlong yacht.

Youngster yuppie
yawns and yields
yummy yerba.

Trace these jokes and then write them on your own:

Where do dogs park their cars? In the barking lot.

When can you know that a vampire has a cold? He starts coffin.

The English language becomes richer by a new word every two hours. The editors of the popular English-language Oxford English Dictionary have estimated that the English vocabulary increases by around 4,000 new words every year. This means that a new word appears on average every two hours!

Use your super creativity and write a one-sentence short story using the word **"YITTEN."***

*YITTEN means frightened in Northern England dialect.

Solve this puzzle and say it out loud!

A	B	C	D	E	F	G	H	I	J	K	L	M
8	7	11	15	13	21	24	5	6	23	17	9	16

N	O	P	Q	R	S	T	U	V	W	X	Y	Z
19	4	10	20	1	14	12	2	3	26	22	25	18

25 4 2 19 24   25 4 9 8 19 15 8   25 8 12 13 14

9 4 3 13 14   25 13 9 9 4 26   25 4 25 4 14

25 4 24 2 1 12   8 19 15

Extra page in case you want to practice some more!

You dig the world's deepest hole. What lies at the bottom? Use cursive and at least 5 words beginning with the letter "Y" in your text...

...and draw a funny illustration!

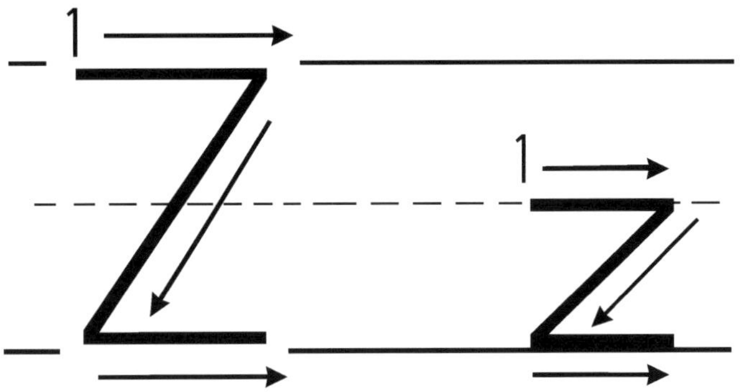

Trace and write the letters:

Z

z

Now let's practice some more:

Ze

Zn

Zu

zz zz zz

za za za

zo zo zo

zh zh zh

Time for short words - let's dive in!

Zoom Zoom Zoom

Zeal Zeal Zeal

Zone Zone Zone

zit zit zit

zen zen zen

zoo zoo zoo

zap zap zap

My neighbor and I have a secret way of communicating, we leave each other hidden notes with handwritten messages. I am always so excited on the way back home from school, as I know there will be something waiting for me! (Audrey, age 11)

Trace these funny sentences and then write them on your own!

Zippy zombie likes zebra zigzags zoo zone.

Zany zoologist has zygomorphic zyst.

Trace these jokes and then write them on your own:

What is the name of a polar bear bank? A snow bank!

What is an insect's favorite sport? Cricket!

A sentence containing all the letters of the alphabet is called a pangram. An example of a well-known English pangram is: "The quick brown fox jumps over a lazy dog."

Use your super creativity and write a one-sentence short story using the word "**ZAZZY.**"*

*ZAZZY means shiny or flashy, for example: zazzy shoes.

Solve this puzzle and say it out loud!

A	B	C	D	E	F	G	H	I	J	K	L	M
5	12	19	13	17	4	9	16	26	3	8	15	24

N	O	P	Q	R	S	T	U	V	W	X	Y	Z
2	20	18	21	10	22	11	25	6	7	23	1	14

___ ___ ___ ___ ___ ___   ___ ___ ___ ___ ___
14 26 14 14 26 22   14 26 18 18 1

___ ___ ___ ___ ___ ___   ___ ___ ___ ___
14 26 18 18 17 10   14 26 18 22

Extra page in case you want to practice some more!

If you could keep any animal as a pet, which one would you choose? Why? Use cursive and at least 5 words beginning with the letter "Z" in your text...

...and draw a funny illustration!

Woooohooo! Isn’t that crazy! Look at you!

Now you’re a real Queen of Print Handwriting and you can even write a beautiful: "Handwriting is my new life passion! I love it!" Isn’t it beautiful?

Come on, let’s have even more fun! Write it down!

And if you want to practice a little more, check out our other books!

Made in the USA
Columbia, SC
22 January 2025

52237619R00089